PERFECT
STRANGER
from Top To
BOTTOM!!!

PERFECT STRANGER
from Top To BOTTOM!!!

HAROLD ARTHUR MORGAN JR

XULON PRESS

Xulon Press
2301 Lucien Way #415
Maitland, FL 32751
407.339.4217
www.xulonpress.com

Due to the changing nature of the Internet, if there are any
web addresses, links, or URLs included in this manuscript,
these may have been altered and may no longer be
accessible. The views and opinions shared in this book
belong solely to the author and do not necessarily reflect
those of the publisher. The publisher therefore disclaims
responsibility for the views or opinions expressed within
the work.

Unless otherwise indicated, Scripture quotations taken
from the King James Version (KJV) – public domain.

Paperback ISBN-13: 978-1-66286-553-4
Ebook ISBN-13: 978-1-66286-554-1

Overview

A Perfect Stranger

THERE IS HOPE for those struggling with addiction! I am a witness to that fact!

Once you quit drinking or using, your work has just begun. Then you need the Spirit of Christ to break the insanity of doing the same thing repeatedly, expecting different results! Once your addiction is fed, the appetite spirals out of control. Christ's Spirit is the solution! "Trust in the Lord with all thine heart and lean not to your own understanding; in all thy ways acknowledging Him and He shall direct thy paths" (Prov. 3:5–6).

First Hint
Jericho

FIRST CORINTHIANS 15:46 says, "That was not first which is spiritual; but that which is natural and afterward that which is spiritual." Generally, we do first that which is natural; we eat three meals a day, get an education to get a good paying job, marry because we're taught to find a wife, have kids, and raise a family. We already have a house because we're taught that we should get a college degree. It is the American dream, but we left God out of the plans.

The Bible states, "Seek ye first the Kingdom of God, and His righteousness and all these things would be added unto you" (Matt. 6:33). It also says, "Trust in the Lord with all thine hears; and lean no to thine own understanding! In all thy ways acknowledge Him, and He shall direct thy paths" (Prov. 3:5–6).

But that's natural if everything goes according to plans, which they usually don't pan out because we forget about putting Christ first in our lives. Those who are usually in worse shape than those plans don't work out. They usually think, "My own power or brains got me to this wealth."

"But thou shall remember the Lord they God; for it is He that giveth the **Power** to get wealth, the He may establish his

1

Covenant which he sware unto they fathers, as it is this day" (Deut. 8:18, emphasis added).

> Now Jericho was straightly shut up because of the children of Israel: **none went out, and none came in.** And the Lord said unto Joshua, "See I have given into thine hand Jericho and the King thereof, and the mighty men of valor. And ye shall compass the city, all ye men of war, and go round about the city once, this shalt thou do six days. And seven priests shall bear before seven trumpets of horns; and the seventh day ye shall compass the city seven times, and the priests shall blow with trumpets. And it shall come to pass, that when they make a long blast with the rams horns, and when ye hear the sound of the trumpet, all the people shall shout with a great shout; and the wall of the city shall fall down flat, and the people shall ascend up every man straight before Him" (Josh. 6:1–5, emphasis added)

We're not bad people trying to be good; we're sick people trying to get well! "But when Jesus heard that, He said unto them, they that be whole need not a physician; **but they that are sick**" (Matt. 9:12).

Then comes addiction, which everybody has because He says in Revelation 21:7, "He the overcometh shall inherit all things; and I will be his God and he shall be my son." Everyone is sick to some extent, enough to cause the second death; *but he that overcometh* shall inherit all things. It happens through the Spirit of the Word of God or Christ!

Jericho is a spot you don't want to be involved in. It is a place where you are cut off from God and Christ. In it is every kind of sickness that Christ healed. None went in, and none came in, and it is every disease that self-will run riot or self-centeredness could offspring.

When God wants to come in, people have their walls up; Christ demands a transformation and sacrifice that would negate all of what they are used to. "It's not by might nor by power, but by my Spirit says the Lord of Host" (Zech. 4:6).

The first things we learn are the ways of the flesh; like me, being born without parents and orphaned from birth!

First Hint

I HAD SUCH a low self-esteem; I was shy, an introvert, and a recluse!

At first, I hated my parents, but some years later, when I was older, I realized they didn't abort me or throw me in a dumpster; they left me in a place where I could be found, and for all of those reasons, I saw the positive. The most they could have done was to raise me to be a man, and here I am, at the age of sixty-four, and writing about recovery. "When my father and mother forsake me, the Lord will take me up" (Ps. 27:10).

Jericho represents all those who are not open-minded. My father was a Baptist! But what are you going to do with your gambling addictions? What are you going to do about your alcohol and drug abuse? What are you going to do about your sex addiction? What are you going to do about your food addiction?

Jericho represents those who are cut off from the Spirit and God's salvation! You might have been sexually abused. "For with God nothing shall be impossible" (Luke 1:37). With men, addictions are beyond your control, which leaves you hopeless!

Jericho is beyond hope because of the walls you've put up. The walls must come down. The Spirit itself is God through Christ.

Jericho is total isolation apart from the Father, which is Christ; in isolation part from God because you know better than the Spirit making you an anti-Christ. Therefore, our walls must come down.

Jericho proves that we are our own worst enemy! "For all that is in the world: the lust of the flesh, the lust of the eyes, and the pride of life, is not of the father; but is of the world" (1 John 2:16).

Our understanding guides us in our youth: the lust of the flesh, eating three meals a day, the lust of the eyes, desiring whatever looks good to you in the world as you go after it, the pride of life, or holding a position in the world.

"But thou shalt remember the Lord thy God, for it is he that giveth thee power to get wealth."

The first hint of these things coming upon us should be a red flag. "I want what I want, and I wanted it yesterday!" The natural man comes first, which leads us to sin or not follow the ways of God. "He that is not with me is against me, he that gathereth not with me scattereth abroad" (Matt. 12:30).

Bottom's Up

ADDICTION IS WHAT keeps us leaning to our own understanding! My best thinking brought me to acute drinking and use because it is the easier, softer way than facing reality. I would rather drink and use, which always results in jail time, institutions, and death, the second death! "This I say then walk in the Spirit; and ye shall not fulfill the lust of the flesh. For the flesh lusted against the Spirit, and the Spirit against the flesh and these are contrary one to the other; so that ye cannot do the things that ye would" (Gal. 5:16–17).

God wants to teach us spirituality for an eternal life, serenity, and love, but we want to escape reality and everything that will lift the pain and our acute situation.

The bottom is next that was not first, which is spiritual, but that which is natural and afterward that which is spiritual.

Our natural life is what we learn from the world; we learn that we are to be the expert in our own destiny. "Be somebody; make a name for yourself." "Work hard, and go after your dream!" The insanity of it all is that the more you get, the bigger your desire is for the flesh, world, and anger because these things and stuff do not satisfy us! Most, well, not most because the Word says, "Many are called but few are chosen" (Matt. 22:18)

"A just man falleth seven times and riseth again up" (Prov. 24:16).

Drinking and using have become acute, leading us to cirrhosis of the liver and other complications. When you live in Jericho, you are shut up; *no one came in; and none went out!* But there is hope for alcoholics and drug addicts; it is when drugs and alcohol increase the acute pain that the saved ask for help by seeking help for their spiritual issue!

Jericho is like "Bottom's Up" drinking and using, and they hurt our family and loved ones. We steal; "the thief cometh not for but to steal, kill and destroy. I have come that they might have life and that more abundantly" (John 10:10).

For us to stop the madness of insanity, many have low self-esteem, real ideal!

Until we reach complete defeat, there is no recovery but a loss of the soul, which is the second death; God show them taking control of your own life and make ourselves God, but this is dangerous. That is the natural way we are taught growing up.

The Lord protected me when I was using. I got my right kidney shot out in 1983. I continue because, "He hath mercy upon whom he will have mercy and upon whom he will hardens" (Rom. 9:18).

A mind is a terrible thing to waste, but the addiction lies and says, "Use one more time; I will solve all of your problems." So, we redouble our willpower to mix, manage, and control our drinking and using. In my case, I got deeper into crack and the bottle!

We willingly try to check ourselves into treatment, and after so many days to detox, we are let go. After my treatment, I found myself going around the friends I used and drank with. Within no time, I was drunk and high again! Then I realized that every time I used crack, I could not perform. After trying countless times, I knew I could not do it. I was envious of people who could manage it since I could not. Why not me? This puzzled me for almost 20 years.

I had stolen twice and was in and out of jails. I checked into an inpatient treatment for thirty days and completed the program.

I forgot to mention I married in Houston, Texas. She was nineteen, and I was twenty-seven. I got a job at Trailways Greyhound for three years. This is where I found crack cocaine; after I got out of high school, they said I sounded white; my life's journey was to be black and find what black means to me!

At that time, I was authoring a book, and I had divorced my wife after 3 ½ years of marriage! She would not make house with me; she stayed around her people and would not cut the apron strings. We had two boys and a girl. I knew I would have raised them, so I divorced and left the kids with her. I went to Phoenix, Arizona, where I was authoring this book because a company in San Diego wanted it, but when I got there, the Lord told me he wanted me to preach it.

So, I scrapped the whole idea. That is the place I originally found crack.

Jericho is like that. Instead of getting in there and fighting for my cause, I found it was going to be tough raising my children, so I decided to scrap the marriage! It was easy for me to leave as I'd never been in one place too long anyway, and my wife gave me the perfect excuse! So, I took it, and now I was free from commitment! Now I wonder where my children are. We had gone to Jackson where I was a kid before I went to Phoenix.

Jericho is when you don't finish what you started; you leave it to someone else and wonder later. That's the insanity of it all; finding my drug of choice to pacify the lack of responsibility in giving up my kids.

Jericho was you doing your best work on the job, even though it was worse because you needed your drug of choice to put you in the mood for work.

Jericho is when you seek or ask for help because insanity says that when using or drinking, you can manage it, even when everyone around you is saying you need to get help. You are in denial!

Denial is the one thing you must be open about in the beginning of recovery; it's our blind spot! People have denied or rejected Christ in many ways, but the main thing they're in denial of is Christ! They deny their flesh through fasting and prayer! They will not miss one meal and drink liquids for Christ's sake. They eat and drink as they did before they came to Christ!

Denial tries to undermine spiritual information by rejecting the Spirit of God that is in Christ! Your using or drinking wasn't that bad; you can use more of me.

Denial happens when the opportunity arises to witness, but I do not speak up. I blow God off because of self-will run riot! My using and drinking takes precedence over everything.

Denial happens when enablers, through self-pity, keep your using and drinking alive when you run out of money; they okay it because they think you have the will power to quit! Little do they know that you are past the state of will power. You are in full blown addiction; past that stage, cravings kick in, and you are off to the races again on a binger or run.

So, we raised the bottom up to show them we had the pattern long before our drinking started or using had started.

My shyness kept me sick. I did not know that I was so introverted till later, but a couple of cans of beer, Colt 45–24 oz, would give me the power to talk to strangers; this cycle kept me sick. When I could stop, I didn't.

Soon, I would find something that made me bottom out, crack cocaine. It was quick-hitting, and I loved the way it made me feel. Let me tell you what happened. When I hit the pipe, it immediately made me paranoid. I dare not move; I was stuck on stupid.

Out of money, they kicked me out of the place where I was using; I would get a hit and go somewhere alone with myself and use. I finally found a drug I loved; I love crack cocaine! I'm glad God kept me from needles or meth. When I used crack, I did not usually drink till I had finished my first love every time I got a piece of money. It went to the dope man! I had switched addictions from beer to crack. In euphoria, I had escaped reality and into my own little world; so, I found it first in Phoenix, Arizona, after I had divorced my first wife.

When I couldn't be assertive, I'd run to crack instead of finding whatever problem or some emotional pain. Crack gave that escape till I no longer needed any excuse. I just wanted it all the time. I reached addiction! I would do anything to get my fix after jails and institutions. I wanted to die using, and several bottoms later, I could not live with it or without it. I admitted defeat!

Introduce Myself

I INTRODUCED MYSELF while being in recovery. I switched addictions after being clean for fourteen years and went back out for two months. I felt the addiction pattern coming back, so I quit. I was a year clean from crack cocaine during the middle of August 2021. I switched back to beer, not hard alcohol. I started with two cans of 24 ounces of Colt 45, and then it shortly later became four cans! I told my counselor I had relapsed on beer. He got me into an outpatient treatment intensive program. At first, I was angry at him, deciding that I really did need help, but I hated admitting defeat. I told him I did not want to die drinking.

Afterward, I told him, "You fooled me, but it's okay," and gave him a hug. I, Harold Arthur Morgan Jr., is in recovery!

Admitting defeat is the start on the road to recovery; I admit I'm out of control. I cannot control alcohol or drugs. We started in Jericho; straight up from being straightly shut up because of the children of Israel. Addiction leaves you cut off from God and Christ. The substance becomes your God.

We all must admit defeat to run our lives because we are flesh, and that's all we know till we are adolescents. Many people are raised by single-parent homes or broken homes.

I was born an orphan into this world in Flint, Michigan, and given over to the state when I was two years old. I slowly migrated west toward St. Joseph's Home for Children in 1969. In 1971, my time was up because I was fourteen years old. They said I had to find some other place to continue. I asked what was available for me. They said Boystown. I got the pamphlet and said yes. So, they made me type my own letter of invitation, then asked me what I was bringing to the table.

About three months later, I was accepted into Boystown, so they flew me from Detroit, Michigan, to Omaha, Nebraska. In August 1971, I was in Omaha, Nebraska, at Boystown.

I graduated high school in January 1975. I went to Midland College in Fremont, Nebraska. Over that summer, I smoked more hash and weed while listening to Elton John. I did not know what I wanted to do, so I dropped out of college. I had a car, and the only thing was to get a job, which I did.

As I said before, I was still for a job but working at Little Kings. After work, we went to the "Joker." But after two or three beers, I would ask Nikki Minaj to dance. I found that after two or three drinks, I would have the courage; this was going to work!

"Be not as a horse or as a mule, which have no understanding: whose mouth must be held in with a bit and bridle lest they come near unto thee" (Ps. 32:9).

> And I turned and lifted mine eyes and looked, and behold, there came four chariots out from between two mountains; and

the mountains were mountains of brass. In the first chariot were red horses; and in the second chariot black horses; and in the third chariot white horses; and in the fourth chariot grizzled and bay horses. Then I answered and said unto the angel that talked with me, what are these my Lord? And the angel answered and said unto me, these are four spirits of the heavens, which go forth from standing before the Lord of all the earth. The black horses, which are therein, go forth into the North Country; and the white horses go forth after them; and grizzled went forth toward the South Country and the bay went forth and sought to go that they might walk to and fro through the earth, and he said, get you hence, walk to and fro through the earth. Then cried he upon me, and spake unto me saying, behold, these that go toward the North Country have quieted my spirit in the North Country (Zech. 6:1–8).

This passage talks about the end-time race before it starts. Four spirits are spoken of, and these represent the race of color. The North Country represents victory over the wild nature. Zechariah was given this revelation of the order of the race at this time. This picks up again in Revelation 6:1–8, which is the order of the race. We were broken late, but not too late to accomplish his purpose.

Now we are in his perfect will. Now there are two horses that will make it to the North Country. The black horses come in first, which represent the black people. The white horses represent the white people. The mountains represent scaling the holy mountain or God through forty days and forty nights of fasting. Non-stop brass represents value; this is also a race for the crown.

Even though Zechariah predicted the race and its finish, it's now happening at this present time.

The order of the horses is important. The present race has two races of people in it. As we look at Revelation 6:1–8, the white horse is in the front, and the black horse is in third place, but it will not end this way. God has two pennies down on that black horse. God is going to prove before our very eyes, "the last shall be first and first shall be last. For many are called, but few are chosen" (Matt. 20:16).

"Come unto me all ye that labor and are haven laden, I will give you rest. Take my yolk upon you and learn of me. For I am meek and lowly in heart. And ye shall find rest unto your souls; for my yolk is easy and my burden is light" (Matt. 11:28–30).

"Therefore, God has mercy on whom he wants to have mercy, and he hardens whom he wants to harden" (Rom. 9:18). He said, "A man's gift maketh room for him and bringeth him before great men" (Prov. 18:16). He also said, "He that overcometh shall inherit all things; and I will be his God; and he shall be my son" (Rev. 21:7).

Jericho, you have shut and cut yourself off from God and shall be destroyed that without a remedy (Prov. 6:15).

"For my thoughts are not your thoughts, neither are your ways, my ways saith the Lord. For as the heavens are higher than the earth, so are my ways higher than your ways, and my thoughts than your thoughts" (Isa. 55:8–9).

Like addiction, we run on self-will run riot; our thoughts are not his thoughts or ways. Until addiction is defeated, there is no hope for recovery. Defeated by addiction, we need the spirit of honesty, open-mindedness, and willingness to gaining a power to restore us back to sanity and also from horsing around to brokenness!

> And I will set my glory among the heathen, and all the heathen shall see my judgement that I have executed, and my hand that I have laid upon them. So, the house of Israel shall know that I am the Lord their God from that day forward. And the heathen shall know that the house of Israel went into captivity for their iniquity: Because they trespassed against me, therefore hid I my face from them, and gave them into the hand of their enemies; so fell they all by the sword. According to their uncleanness and according to their

trespasses have I done unto them and hid my
face from them (Ezek. 39:21–24).

But Jesus testified that the second coming of Christ would
not be him; He handled the day. "Jesus said I must work the
work of him that sent me while it is day for the night cometh
when no man can work! No flesh will work but an angel will:
I Jesus have sent mine angel to testify unto you these things
in the churches; I am the root and offspring of David; and the
bright and morning star."

The seventh angel is what Revelation is all about. The seventh angel is doing it all; from transformation to transformation, from substance abuse to angel.

The second coming Christ is Jesus's angel! Walk in the
United States, and the angel's name is Lightning! "For as
the lightening cometh out of the East and shineth even
unto the West; so shall also the coming of the son of man be"
(Matt. 24:27).

> "For as the lightning, that lighteneth out of
> the one part under heaven, shineth unto the
> other part under heaven; so shall the son of
> man be in his day" (Luke 17:27).
> "I beheld Satan as lightning fall from heaven"
> (Luke 10:18).
> And behold, there was a great earthquake, for
> an angel of the Lord descended from heaven
> and came and rolled back the stone and sate

on it. His appearance was like lightning, and his clothing white as snow. And for fear of him the guards trembled and became like dead men. But the angel said to the women, "Do not be afraid, for I know that you seek Jesus who was crucified. He is not here, for he has risen, as he said. Come, see the place where he lay. Then go quickly and tell his disciples that he has risen from the dead, and behold, he is going before you to Galilee; there you will see him. See, I have told you" (Matt. 28:2–7).

Now the time has come to stop horsing around. Know that the horse must be broken before you can ride him, and even then, he must have a bit bridle.

In Revelation 6:1–8 is the updated standings of the race as of the year 2000 AD. The black horse is back in third position in verses 5 and 6; we found that out. When the first four seals were open, then appeared the horse of prophecy of Zechariah in progress.

Seemingly a long shot back in third place, this is the greatest closing horse of all time. That is why has a two-penny investment in the horse. He has the balances in the race. It's for all the marbles. Lightning on his own beast will win by seven lengths a blowout! And a hundred and forty-four thousand will be with Lightning when he comes in from substance abuse to animal to angel, the three stages.

"I beseech you brethren, by the mercies of God, that ye present your bodies a living sacrifice, holy, acceptable unto God, which your reasonable service. And be not conformed to this world: but be ye transformed by the renewing of your mind, that ye may prove what is that good, and acceptable, and perfect, will of God" (Rom. 12:1–2).

The culmination of Zechariah 6:1–8 is Revelation 14:1–5. There will be a lot of cussing. These also will not defile with women, for they are virgins.

"And I looked, and, lo, a Lamb stood on the mount Sion, and with him an hundred forty and four thousand, having his Father's name written in their foreheads" (Rev. 14:1).

This victory comes as the hundred and forty-four thousand follow the Lamb forty days and forty nights, which the fasting was put on their foreheads by the Lamb himself to scale the holy mountain of God, Mount Sion. "Be not overcome of evil; but over evil with good" (Rom. 12:21).

"And in the mouth was found no guile for there without fault before the throne of God" (Rev. 14:5).

He hasn't forgot the Black race; the time has come full circle and his people he foreknew and gave them time served. Remember Zechariah 6:6. The Black horse comes first unto the North Country, and the White horse goes after them.

Christ's Holy Mount Sion must be conquered first, and for forty days and forty nights, not a bite of food can be taken at all, only plain water and liquids. There is more I would tell a perfect stranger about Jericho, and, in addition, we will see you on the top of Mount Sion with me. "God has mercy upon whom He will have mercy and upon who he will be hardeneth" (Rom. 9:18).

Jericho Again

BUT HE, WILLING to justify himself, said unto Jesus, and who is my neighbor? And Jesus answering said, "a certain man went down from Jerusalem to Jericho and fell amount thieves, which stripped him of his raiment, and wounded him, and departed leaving him half dead. And by chance there came down a certain priest, that way; and when he saw him, he passed by on the other side. And likewise, a Levite, when he was at the place; came and look on him, he passed by on the other side. But a certain Samaritan, as he journeyed, came where he was: and when he saw him, he had compassion on him. And went to him, and bound-up his wounds, pouring in oil and wine, and set him on his own beast. And brought him to an inn and took care of him. And on the morrow when he departed, he took out two pence, and gave them to the host, and said unto him, 'take care of him; and whatsoever thou spendest more, when I come again, I will repay thee.' Which now these three thinkest thou were neighbor to him that fell among thieves?" And he said, "he that shewed mercy on him"; then said Jesus unto him, "go and do thou likewise" (Luke 10:29–37).

What would I tell the perfect stranger? It all starts when addiction defeats us and has been our master. We lose our future selves upstairs. Insanity is all we are running on.

Upstairs – "For my thoughts are not your thoughts, neither are your ways my ways, saith the Lord. "For as the heavens are higher than the earth, so are my ways higher than your ways, and my thoughts than your thoughts" (Isa. 55:8–9).

In "First Hint," we learn that Jericho is like an addiction; we do not want anything or anybody inside the walls we put up. Our addiction becomes so acute that only a power can bring them down because we are cut off from our God, the ending being jails, institutions, and death.

Some people must die for others to live. Jericho was defeated, the wall came down, and we couldn't hide our addictions any longer. We had to admit the consequences. We had hit bottom.

The people we hurt, the relationships we broke, some of our closest friends died, and we still did not get the message; addiction is a sin. When we become extreme with anything, it become our god. "Thou shalt have no other Gods before me."

We learn that we had to start **Upstairs** in our minds. "And be not conformed to this world but be ye transformed by the renewing of your mind that ye may prove what is that acceptable good, and perfect will of God." For our thoughts were not his thoughts, neither were our ways his ways. All you must do is change everything!

The **First Hint** for me was that I ran my own life and forgot good orderly direction or God! It is a case of self-will run riot; nobody can tell me what to do; I make my own decisions. It is my way or the highway! Me all the way! I want what I want and when I want it. **Upstairs:** "Trust in the Lord with all thine heart and lean not to thine own understanding. In all thy ways acknowledge Him and he shall direct thy paths" (Prov. 3:5–6).

The **First Hint** for me was when I got out of high school after working at Little Kings, and we would go to the Joker in Council Bluffs. I was shy and introverted, but after two to three beers, it changed me and gave me courage. I could ask Nikki Minaj to dance. After that, I was ok with drinking; this was my way of an opening with beer and an instant hit. Now I could deal with anything. This was really going to work!

The Wounded Man

WOUND: 1. HURT or injury that cuts skin; 2. to injure the feelings or pride, and 3. any cause of pain or grief as to the feelings or honor.

This is what I get: the wounded man wasn't in a position to ask for help, although he needed special attention. "We that are strong ought to bear the infirmities of the weak, and not to please ourselves" (Rom. 15:1).

"Bear ye one another's burdens, and so fulfill the law of Christ" (Gal. 6:2).

When we share our message of recovery, no matter how critical the situation, our message is that we come to you and let you know we have been there too! In sharing the nature of addiction, we, like Jesus, have a hundred sheep, and when one goes astray as sheep do, Jesus rejoices more for that sheep than the ninety-nine that don't go astray. As sheep, we go astray, but the right shepherd, according to their addiction, knows exactly how we can get lured away with the wrong crowd.

Recovery starts when you let your walls down and find the root cause. Usually, it is self-will, low self-esteem, and pride. "The thief comes only to steal and kill and destroy;

I have come that they may have life and have it to the full" (John 10:10).

He made up his mind to go to Jericho; he knew he was trying a different lifestyle than he was used to! He tried an easier, softer way!

They stripped him of his raiment, leaving him "exposed" or "naked." That's what drugs and alcohol do; they reveal our sick nature, leaving us in a helpless state where people can see our insanity, knowing we're cursed.

When we have been wounded, we're in a state where our very souls are at stake, and the only recovery is by fasting and prayer. It could be a flesh wound or spiritual or emotional wound. To the fragile, both can leave our very souls at stake.

That being so, only a Christ-centered ministry is our hope of salvation. That is what is meant by pouring in oil and wine; the joy of the Lord, with the Spirit of Christ, can only reach people in this condition. It is the only miracle for this type of shame. "Brethren, if a man be overtaken in a fault, ye which are spiritual, restore such a one in the spirit of meekness, considering thyself, lest thou also be tempted" (Gal. 6:1).

Brought him to an inn, where he could get rest and the nature of his beast could be healed.

The personal gratification for this kind of restoration is immensely great because you have given him almost and, in fact, your very own soul through the Spirit. They were both perfect strangers who never saw each other again!

I introduced myself as the one who went through transformation, from addiction to becoming completely sober.

Addiction is so cunning, baffling, and powerful that it takes you receiving the Spirit of Christ to overcome it. "Be not overcome of evil, but overcome evil with good" (Rom. 12:21).

I know I was born to do something great. "I find then a law; when I would do good evil is present with me" (Rom. 7:2). **Upstairs:** "I thank God through Jesus Christ our Lord so with the mind I serve the Lord God, but with the flesh the law of sin" (Rom. 7:25).

Upstairs: " My thoughts are not your thoughts, neither my ways your ways saith the Lord as the heavens are higher than the earth, so are my ways higher than your ways, and my thoughts than your thoughts" (Isa. 55:8–9).

Upstairs: "Till we all come into the unity of the faith, and of the knowledge of the son of God, unto a perfect man, unto the measure of the stature of the fullness of Christ" (Eph. 4:13).

Upstairs: This means to keep the Scripture in your mind; it all starts with Isaiah 55:8–9.

A perfect stranger, if he's able to ask for help, if he's of Christ to fulfill God's will, Jericho didn't ask for help; they were wrapped in themselves and were unholy.

Upstairs: "Follow peace with all men and holiness without which no man shall see the Lord" (Heb. 12:14).

If you are past the breaking point, God's will and able to break your fall. If you know that you need Christ's help, don't delay. Abba Father, let go of your pride, and God will abundantly pardon. Fasting and prayers are key. He said they would be ever learning and never able to come to the knowledge of the truth (2 Tim. 3:7).

"For all that's in the world the lust of the flesh, the lust of the eyes, and the pride of life is not of the Father but is of the world" (1 John 2:16).

The lust of the flesh! You cannot put down food too but continue eating like the rest of the world. Ask yourself if a spirit needs food. Of course, not. That is why we fail to be more connected with the Father through Christ!

"He that believeth on me, as the scripture hath said, out of his belly shall flow rivers of living water. But this spake he of the Spirit, which they that believe on him should receive; for the Holy Ghost was not yet given; because that Jesus was not yet gloried" (John 7:38–39).

Why is all the water urinating out of your belly? It takes forty days and forty nights consecutively to bring in the Spirit of Christ into your belly!

You need to know that being completely sober means you have crossed over to true spirituality. It does not happen overnight because insanity did not come overnight. We have addiction long before it's completely full-blown or are recognizable as a person. Whatever the case may be, becoming or being completely sober is a spiritual matter. Your God—I call my God: Christ—can restore you to sanity or a sound mind. The addiction is only 15 to 20 percent of the problem. Learning how to live a true recovery program takes the rest of your life and time.

Like we said before, learning to forgive yourself will take a good portion of time. The greatest amount of time is used to find the root cause of self-destruction. The behavior surrounding God of our understanding is all **Upstairs**. We must renew our minds, which means we have to get into the Bible! "Because God is not the author of confusion, but of peace, as in all churches of the saints" (1 Cor. 14:33).

A perfect life is a balancing act between our God's chosen way and emotional sobriety. Our lives' task is to cross over from the flesh and into complete sobriety through the gaining of a spiritual, emotional bottom. We all have a spiritual, emotional bottom, and asking for help putting off price is where all recovery starts through sharing! Faith comes by hearing and hearing by the Word of God (Rom. 10:17).

Yet Upstairs

ROMANS 7:25 SAYS, "I thank God through Jesus Christ our Lord; so, with the mind I myself serve the law of God, but with the flesh the law of sin." First Corinthians 15:46 says, "That was not first which is spiritual but that which is natural and afterwards that which is spiritual."

Because I want a mind that is emotional and spiritual, we "need not to be conformed to this world but be ye transformed by the renewing of your mind, that ye may prove what is that good, acceptable, and perfect will of God" (Rom. 12:2).

The Good Samaritan proved what is good; he helped to restore him who fell among thieves who stripped him of his raiment. He went from Jerusalem down to Jericho; people want an easier and softer way than holiness, but the Word says to follow peace with all men and holiness without which no man shall see Lord (Heb. 12:14).

Like we said before, using or drinking alcohol is only 10 to 20 percent of the problem. We were not ready to live on life's term. The raiment was spiritual excellence but not wanting separation from the world, which holiness demands chose what he thought would allow him to take. "Wide is the gate, and broad is the way, that leadeth to destruction, and many there be which go in there at: Because strait is the gate, and narrow is the way, which leadeth unto life, and few there be that find it" (Matt. 7:13–14).

Unless you receive the Spirit of the Father, you are going down. He went from Jerusalem down to Jericho. Jerusalem represents the spiritual city where the righteous live. Are you trying to have Jerusalem and Jericho at the same time? "A double minded man is unstable in all his ways" (James 1:8).

When we struggle with recovery, usually it's because we are seeking mixed messages. People know you go to church, but what is your life like away from church? Moses said, "your sin will find you out."

The more distance natural man leads our spiritual man, the more acute our addiction becomes; we get worse because we are not satisfied with a spiritual lifestyle.

We thought this life was not any fun; the thieves were pride, self-will run riot, and flesh. The flesh is because we keep eating and cannot fast, which is required for the transformation; pride is because we had our own idea of what life and being secure in this life meant. So, we drank or used, and it helped us escape life for a brief period, but the problem did not go away.

Now we were high or drunk and broke and did not pay the bills, but one thing was clear: one more drink will fix it. We tried to escape life but fell deeper and deeper in addiction. We were sure we could manage it to the point that we were drinking and using 24/7!

Because we must process why or what made us do such destructive drinking and using. In Jerusalem security, shelter altogether Heaven; but we didn't want that because we didn't understand Christ's spirit, and how we connect with Him is by fasting.

It doesn't say whether the wounded man got saved or was completely recovered! It doesn't even say whether or not he made it back to Jerusalem or if he was completely made whole or restored! I'm yet upstairs because I want to recover along spiritual lines! "But the Lord was unto them precept upon precept, precept upon precept; line upon line, line upon line; here a little and there a little; that they might go, and fall backward, and be broken, and snared and taken" (Isa. 28:13).

I'm working between my ears and try subject. You have to first subject yourself to God's Word and Spirit! Once you leave the space he's given you, you give place to the devil. **Upstairs:** "Submit yourselves therefore to God: resist the devil and he will flee from you" (James 4:7).

"But be ye doers of the word, not hearers only, deceiving your own selves" (James 1:7).

The more you stray from the light, the darker it gets. Let addiction be called what it is: confusion.

Upstairs: "For God is not the author of confusion; but of peace, as in all the churches of the saints" (1 Cor. 14:33).

Addiction says, "It can't hurt you; use more of me." Loneliness and isolation set in; now you're hooked; it's just one more on top of one more hit of cocaine or one more beer or a pint to oblivion! Addiction strips away all self-worth and will to fight back; now you're at the jump-off point. At this point, it means God's care for us is revealed or jails, institutions, or death!

Upstairs: "The thief cometh not but for to kill, steal and destroy, I am come that they might have life, and have it more abundantly" (John 10:10).

The man that fell among thieves didn't see it coming. Robbed of our willpower, addiction takes centerstage! It was Jericho at its best! We lose sight of all that's decent and right and just—another bottom! This one's not emotional or physical but spiritual!

You've got to be willing to grow along spiritual lines. Now that I am sober, I've got **Upstairs**: "Standfast therefore in the liberty; where with Christ hath made us free, and he not entangled again with the yolk of bondage" (Gal. 5:1)

As long as I stay free from all mind-altering substances and compounds, with fasting, I might just reach my sober quest. When you starve yourself, not eating anything but drinking clear liquids for forty days and nights consecutively, you bring in the goal of worshipping God by receiving Christ! Jesus did it, and he kept his **Upstairs**: "He that hungreth and thirsteth after righteousness shall be filled" (Matt. 5:6). These people are "blessed," the Scripture says! Spirit so full as the law required; going out forty days and nights, three times in a year! Which the males were required to do.

Upstairs: "He that believeth on me as the scripture hath said; out of his belly shall flow rivers of living water!" (John 7:38).

"This spake He of the Spirit; which they that believe on him should receive" (John 7:39).

I'm yet upstairs because of the battles between our ears, our mind. I used this Scripture before—**Upstairs**: "I thank God through Jesus Christ our Lord, so with the mind I myself serve the Law of God; but with the flesh the law of sin" (Rom. 7:25).

We already discuss Jericho as my quest, to cross over from being sober to the Spirit of Salvation, Christ. That's why I'm yet upstairs because I'm trying to grow along spiritual lines, as I've mentioned before.

Upstairs: "For the word of the Lord was unto them precept upon precept; precept upon precept; line upon line, line upon line; here a little and there a little; that they might go and fall backwards and be broken, and snared and taken" (Isa. 28:13).

If we're going to beat addiction and the race of color in Zechariah 6:1–8, while recovering from Jericho's first defeat by our walls coming down. Seeing our true animal, horse, which hath no understanding, we went from Jerusalem to down to Jericho again and fell amount thieves.

Upstairs: "A just man falleth seven times, and riseth up again; but the wicked shall into mischief" (Prov. 24:16).

Jericho was cursed by Joshua in Joshua 6:26: "Cursed be the man before the Lord, that riseth up and buildeth this city Jericho. He shall lay the foundation thereof in his first-born, and his youngest son be set up for the gates of it." His prophesy came true; a man tried to rebuild Jericho, and his oldest son and youngest son died!

We also find in 2 Kings that Jericho had sons of the prophet in the days of Elijah and Elisha (2 Kings 2:4–5, 18; 2 Kings 2:19–22). Elisha healed the waters and said that there shall be no more death nor barren land by throwing through a new cruse of salt. In 2 Chronicles 28:15, certain men of Samaria took from Judah and Jerusalem two hundred thousand men, women, sons, daughters, and the spoil and brought them to Samaria. But God sent Obed the prophet, who rebuked them for taking their brethren for bondmen and bondwomen!

After the rebuke, certain expressed by name took the captives and restored them!

"With the spoil clothed all that were naked among them, and arrayed them, and shod them, and gave them to eat and to drink, and anointed them, and caried all they feeble of them upon asses, and brought them to Jericho, the city of palm trees, to their brethren; then they returned to Samaria" (2 Chron. 28:15).

I'm **Upstairs** because of Romans 12:2: "Be not conformed to this world, but, be ye transformed by the renewing of your mind; so that ye can proved what is that good and acceptable, and perfect will of God."

The real work of recovery is between our ears: our mind! We're trying to grow along spiritual lines; that's what I would tell a perfect stranger. We have to cross over to the true spirit through the King James Version of the Bible.

Upstairs: "But the word of the Lord was unto them precept upon precept, precept upon precept; line upon line, line upon line; here a little and there a little; that they might go, and fall backward and be broken, and snared and taken" (Isa. 28:13).

"For the word is quick and powerful, sharper than any two-edged sword; piercing even to the dividing asunder of soul and spirit; and of the joints and of the marrow, and is a discerner of the thoughts and intents of the heart" (Heb. 4:12). We must be hard on ourselves but considerate of others! That's where fasting and prayer come in; our nature on the inside must be transformed! Forty days and nights of drinking water or clear liquid brings in the crossover Spirit of Christ!

Now we can be like Revelation 14:1–5 and make it to the top of Sion (Mt.), Sion the holy mountain of God. Because we are virgins in the spirit, He made to understand fasting and how it purifies you through your stomach or belly. He has made us kings and priests unto him. "So we ensamples to the flock; not for filthy lucre, but of a ready mind, feed the flock of God which is among taking the oversight thereof; not by constraint, but willingly" (1 Pet. 5:2).

We want to cross over from a self-centered life to a God-centered life! Natural to spiritual! Colorless to colorful! Overnight to oversight! **Upstairs** is an act: "do unto others, as you would have them do unto you! For this is the law and the prophets!" (Matt. 7:12).

Sober Quest

NOW THAT WE'VE got **Upstairs,** the main word that God is trying to reveal to us is to move on to our sober quest. "That probably no human power could have relieved our alcoholism; that God could and would if he were sought." I am sober now, but in order to fully enjoy my newfound sobriety, I have to see the Father, Christ's spirit, within my temple. "For if I build again the things which I destroyed I make myself a transgressor" (Gal. 2:18). "Seek ye first the Kingdom of God and all these things shall be added unto you" (Matt. 6:33). "Now since I'm sober; I find He has mercy on whom he will have mercy and on whom he hardeneth" (Rom. 9:18).

Now my quest is standfast in the liberty wherewith Christ has made us free and not entangled again with the yolk of bondage (Gal. 5:1)! The bondage is from my food addiction; He has shown me that fasting and prayer is the spirit that will deliver from the bondage of the flesh! "God is a spirit and they that worship Him must worship in Spirit and truth" (John 4:24).

He wants me to stand out from the crowd. "Come out from among them, and, be ye separate saith the Lord; touch not the unclean thing and I will receive you!" (2 Cor. 6:17).

This spiritual life comes from dropping the food addiction. Jesus said, "If any man come unto me let him deny himself take up his cross and follow me" (Matt. 16:24).

"For all that is in the world, the lust of the flesh; the lust of the eyes and the pride of life!" (1 John 2:16). The main culprit is the lust of the flesh. When your stomach growls because you are hungry, you eat right away, and that's usually meat, which is the only unclean thing that stops the drawing up of your spirit. We must be converted to the spirit's lifestyle. That's how you standfast in the liberty wherewith Christ hath made us free and be not entangled again with the yolk bondage (Gal. 5:1).

"For by one Spirit are we all baptized into one body whether we be Jews or Gentiles, whether we be bond or free; and have all been made to drink into the one spirit" (1 Cor. 12:13).

"If we live in the Spirit, let's also walk in the Spirit" (Gal. 5:28).

Remember, the main culprit that blocks the spirit is meat!

Animals welcome my recent past; I horsed around a lot. Alcohol and drugs took up a huge chunk of my life, and I didn't like my reality. This is my third book I'm writing, saying that through sober living, I have crossed over to the Spirit walk with God! My quest is to make it to the top of Mount Sion (Rev. 14:1–5); this is still yet to come. "Confess your fault one to another and pray ye one for another that ye may be healed, the effectual fervent prayer of a righteous man availeth much!" (James 5:16). "A just man falleth seven times and riseth up again; but the wicked will fall into mischief" (Prov. 24:16).

I hit my bottoms because of horsing around. Zechariah 6:1–8 is the prophesy of the race. God has given me insight into the race. Two horses will come in, and the color of the horse denotes the nationality and race of people. The black horse denotes the nationality and race of people, the black horse that comes in first is the black race, and the white race or horse comes forth after them (Zech. 6:6). This is in the recent future. "Be not as the horse or mule, which hath no understanding; who's mouth must be held in, with bit and bridal lest they come nigh thee!" (Ps. 32:9).

"All we like sheep have gone astray we've all turned and gone our own way and the Lord hath laid on him the iniquity of us all" (Isa. 53:6). That's why Christ had to come to end the law and bring in grace. In Acts 10:9–16, Peter saw a vision; animals in a vessel knit at the four corners. Peter had to be shown the Gentiles and that the opening of the door would be given to him. "What God has cleansed that call not that common. The vessel was let down three times and lifted back up into heaven" (Acts 10:16).

He is showing me that you can stay animals but make peace with him first through fasting and prayer, which changes the internal nature! "Be not conformed to this world but be ye transformed by the renewing of your mind; that ye may prove what is that good, acceptable, and perfect will of God" (Rom. 12:2).

Not only has it come nigh me, but you can't beat a dead horse, which is me turning into a lamb (Rev. 14:1).

After taking the race, we'll gather 144,000 black men in the process and having our Father's name written in their foreheads (Rev. 14:1).

I've been sober for eighty-three days now, but my quest is to take the oversight and feed the flock of God, which he purchased with his own blood; not by constraint, but of a ready mind (1 Pet. 5:2).

One day at a time, I'm going to fast until I reach the place where I am supposed to go.

It means doing unto others as I would have them do unto me, the Golden Rule; this is the law and the prophets. The people that understand the book are blessed! The crossover: Romans 12:21: "Be not overcome of evil but overcome evil with good!" Take the oversight by crossing over through fasting. "I beseech you therefore brethren by the mercies of God, that ye present your bodies as a living sacrifice, Holy acceptable unto God; which is your reasonable service!" (Rom. 12:1).

One day at a time, I lift my soul to Christ as an offering that he may consume! "For our God is a consuming fire" (Heb. 12:29).

The oversight is being hard on ourselves but considerate of others. It's a dark world right now, and nobody is trying to seek the Father but me, although I'm not good at it yet! I'm fasting presently

Sober Quest
Jericho Followed Christ

"AND AS THEY departed from Jericho, a great multitude followed Him!" (Matt. 20:29).

"And they came to Jericho; and as he went out of Jericho with his disciples and a great number of people, blind Bartimaeus, the son of Timaeus sat by the highway side begging (Mark 10:46).

"And it came to pass, that as he was come night unto Jericho, a certain blind main sat by the way side begging" (Luke 18:35).

"And Jesus entered and passed through Jericho, and behold, there was a man name Zacchaeus, which was the chief among publicans, and he was rich" (Luke 19:1–2).

The modern-day Jericho in Jesus's day was the only city that followed his will such that with the Father, there was a multitude to follow him, not like the Old Testament Jericho; they were waiting for Him. They had such faith that Jesus didn't have to work any miracle throughout the city proper. He did miracles before he entered Jericho and after he left Jericho. Jericho has evolved from the Old Testament to the New Testament; the walls are completely down forever.

Sought Out
Jericho Key

GOD COULD AND would if He were sought! Why is Jericho key? It was the only city ready to follow God by faith. None were feeble; His presence alone was enough. The Jericho multitude, also known as the Jericho call, were ready to step out in faith like Abraham. They left, not knowing where Christ would lead them, but He was sought by them.

What an amazing praise! They recognized His presence and acknowledged His deity, which was a far cry from Jericho in the beginning, which had to be utterly destroyed; the walls, their security, had to be smashed and established.

He entered and departed; no miracles in the city proper. He started an everlasting bond with Jericho, and at the days end, they followed Christ.

He was sought by them, then left, knowing that he was sought out. "Come unto me all ye that labor and are heavy laden, I will give you rest. Take my yok upon you and learn of me, for I am meek and lowly at heart; and ye shall find rest unto your souls formerly yolk is easy and burden is light" (Matt. 11:28–30).

Sought Out
Jericho Call

HE ENTERED JERICHO and departed from Jericho. "Seek ye first the Kingdom of God and His righteousness and all these things will be added unto you" (Matt. 6:33).

This is the crossover: "that was not first which is spiritual, but that which is natural and afterward that which is spiritual" (1 Cor. 15:46).

"Crossing over" is the deepest you can get in the Spirit. "Be not overcome of evil but over to me evil with good!" (Rom. 12:21).

"Confess your faults one to another and pray ye one for another that ye may be healed, the effectual fervent prayer of a righteous man availeth much" (James 5:16).

"He that cometh to me and hate not his father, mother, wife, kids yea; and his only life also he cannot be my disciple!" (Luke 14:26).

"And whosoever beareth not his cross and cometh after me cannot be my disciple" (Luke 14:27).

"So likewise, whosoever of you that forsaketh not all that hath cannot be my disciple" (Luke 14:33).

The Jericho call brought out multitudes of people who dropped everything and followed Him.

SOUGHT OUT
Jericho Key

JERICHO IS KEY because of its transformation! After Elisha healed the waters and said there would be no more barren land, as I stated before, Jericho became a key work. Elijah was sent to Jericho. Elisha tarried awhile in Jericho with the sons of the prophets. Jericho and Evangelist dream, Jesus led them out. He entered Jericho and passed through Jericho. He did no miracles in the city proper, but nigh unto Jericho, he did miracles; blind Bartimaeus, and after he left Jericho, Zacchaeus. "If we live in the Spirit let us also walk in the Spirit! (Gal. 5:25).

"Not by might nor by power; but, by my Spirit saith the word of the Lord unto Zerubbabel!" (Zech. 4:6).

The "Crossing over" be not overcome of evil but overcome evil with good (Rom. 12:21).

We learn one day a time—"Do unto others, as you would have them do unto you" (Matt. 7:12).

Jericho will always be the city that turned it all around, a city of great faith. "Just like Enoch, who walked with God and was not for God took him; the seventh from Adam" (Gen. 5:24).

Sought Out

Jericho's Testimony

JERICHO HAS A testimony, the only city that has no blemishes. Jesus didn't have to do any miracles on the sick, palsy or anything. He just walked right though Jericho; I want to be like Jericho, which didn't need to be reprimanded. No chastisement, a city up to date with the Lord; the hospitality was right, and no demons were in the city. Those who need physicians are those who are sick. I came not to call the righteous but sinners to repentance!

All we know about that Jericho then is that multitudes followed him. No sermons were preached in Jericho or devils cast out in the city proper. Consider how great this city is; it's boggling. There were no curses, no blind individuals in the city proper, and no diseases to speak of. The city was a role model for us today; no movements started; no children sick to speak of, and he didn't have to show his power in any way! There was not a feeble one among them. He just passed right through. No leaders were degraded, and everyone who was supposed to follow Him did! There was nobody out of order. Jericho was a clean bill of health. There was no insanity or mental illness, which completely made up for Jericho in Joshua's day. There were no addictions; everyone was in place!

I want to follow Jericho's testimony; they were ready when Jesus came. There were no people to visit and nobody trying to make him King or trying to touch Him. They accepted Him as Christ. Nobody was out of order, like I said; there were no lectures or speeches, no addictions of any kind, no people to pray for, and no laying on of hands.

"These six things doth the Lord hate: yea seven are abomination unto Him; A proud look, a lying tongue, and hands the shed innocent blood, an heart that deviseth wicked imaginations, feet that be swift in running to mischief, a false witness that speaketh lies, and he that soweth discord amount brethren" (Prov. 6:16–19). None of the things were found in Jericho. His righteousness would have cried out against it. In the presence of God, every knee shall bow, every tongue must confess that Jesus Christ is Lord, to the glory of God the Father (Eph. 2:10–11)!

"He that hath been baptized into Christ, hath put on Christ" (Gal. 3:27).

Once you are in Christ, His Spirit purges you from all unrighteousness! Jericho had it, "for ye are not in the flesh but in the Spirit; if so be that the Spirit of God dwells in you, now if any many have not the Christ he is none of His" (Rom. 8:9).

Last Laugh

LAUGH'S BEST, I switched addictions from crack cocaine to beer, and the same loss of control happened again. My sponsor helped me get back into treatment after I told him I had relapsed on beer. After I completed the intensive outpatient treatment, I received a certificate. I'm level 1 now. The Lord showed me if I'd fast, not only would he cure me but he'd also give me the message of addiction, and I would also get the laugh last over all my enemies, and he'd make me the head and not the tail. "The last shall be first and the first last; because many are called but few are chosen" (Matt. 20:16).

Our stories disclose in a general way, what we used to be like, what happened, and what we are like now.

I was born an orphan and given over to the state of Michigan when I was two years old. I remember being in a foster home first.

I used to get in trouble with the other kids in the house. They would rip up my sheets and say I did it. My foster dad had one arm, and the other arm was an artificial arm. He sure knew how to give whippings. I ran away from home after the family that wanted to adopt me didn't because I had an asthma attack that scared them, so they didn't want me! When I ran away, God led me right to the house at that young age!

After they took me back, I got a whipping! I complained to my social worker that I didn't like where I was staying, and after almost three years, they put me in the University of Michigan's campus. It was called CPH, Children's Psychiatric Hospital, a temporary placement.

After two years, I went to Jackson, Michigan, to St. Joseph's Home for Boys; later after they started taking in girls. St. Joseph's Home for Children Felician Sisters ran the place; it was Catholic. We were still allowed to go to another church called Ganson Street Baptist Church. I liked it because I felt the Spirit moving as the minister brought the Word of God! After I turned fourteen years old, I had to leave that place. I asked them what my options were, and they said Boystown. After I read the pamphlet for Boystown, I decided that's where I wanted to go, and I typed my letter of entrance.

Three months later, they accepted me, and I flew from Detroit, Michigan, to Omaha, Nebraska. I know I had trouble because I was always being uprooted. It was hard for me to keep friends, but I won't forget Leonard Relmierski, a social worker who came to see me regularly. He would buy me ice cream floats when he visited me!

I had asthma really bad when I was young, and I used to take shots every two weeks. I couldn't eat eggs at that time at Boystown, I stopped playing the violin because I thought it was sissy, and my grades were Cs, Bs, and occasionally a D when I was in school.

I was more interested in Protestant Chapel because the preacher there had the Spirit. Way down deep inside, I said, "Lord, if you make me one (minister), I'll show them how it's done."

I played on the gold team, and in my senior year, I was city councilman for Section 3. I beat out a sport's jock by one vote. My theme was "The Little Man with Big Suggestions." I graduated a half year early and was accepted at Midland College.

Over the summer, I spent more time smoking weed and listening to Elton John than anything. I didn't know what I wanted to do, so I dropped out. I was in Fremont at that time, so I came back to Omaha! I worked at Little King's subs sandwich place on 132nd and Center.

Afterward, we would go to the "Joker" in Council Bluffs, Iowa. I was shy, but after a couple of beers, I would ask Nikki Minaj for a dance. It was liquid courage; I found out this would work, so I started drinking beer.

I found beer. Whenever I felt insecure, I would drink. This worked for quite a while. So I went back to Jackson, Michigan.

After I got out of the Navy from January '77 to February '78, my asthma bothered me because of the chemicals on the ship. I was always at sick bay. We used to get shore leave, and as an operational specialist, I operated ship-to-ship communications and radar.

They left me at Guam, where I was given a medical honorable discharge. On shore leave, I'd drink and pick up a girl.

At Jackson, Michigan, I got a good job working at Camshaft Machine Company, making camshafts for engines.

Then I would drink till I got drunk. I bought a car and a house, only I was paying for the house.

I met a girl at the bar; she lived in Lansing, thirty-five miles north of Jackson. On my break, I went home to Jackson and found her in the house with another man. I slapped her, then we made love, but I couldn't trust her, so I took her back to Lansing. I drove all night and day till I came to Omaha, Nebraska. I left that good job and got into trouble right away. I purse-snatched from a plain-clothed nun. I spent a flat year for that, no good time in jail.

Something told me that I had a baby, so I traveled to Lansing again, and I got to see my son, but he had a twitch in his arm. I found his mother doing T's and Blues, where you shoot up in your arm. I got a job and worked in Lansing for a while. I left my son with those foster parents and came back to Omaha.

I went hard after the church United Pentecostal Church, where I ministered but slept with a woman of the night and felt dirty, and he said he would have to sit me down for a year. I felt that was too harsh of punishment, so the woman I had met told me she would marry me only in San Antonio, Texas, so I took the keys to the church, pawned his guitar, took the money, and headed for San Antonio.

When we came to San Antonio, my car overheated. Four guys helped me push the car off the street to the grass. I went to get some oil and water, and when I came back, the girl was gone. Here came these four guys; it was getting dark, and my car wouldn't start. They said they normally get such and such when they help, and I knew they were talking about money.

I said, "Let's go this way to see if we can find the girl."

"Either you're ready, or we're ready," they said.

With a loud voice, I said, "This is all I'm giving you," and I gave each one twenty dollars. I walked back to my car, got in, and with my head on the steering wheel, I looked up, and there were seven of them running for my car. I started my car, and it started, and I drove off, waving goodbye.

I came into Houston off I-10 and hung out for a while, drinking. I tried two jobs but couldn't make the quota. So, a guy let me stay at his place, but I was out of money. So I pawned his tv and came back to the same spot because I didn't know any others. He came into the speakeasy bar, and a fight broke out, so we went outside. I wasn't really fighting back because I knew I was in the wrong.

Something was in the dark off to the right, so I pushed him off me and ran to the right, jumped one fence and thought I'd made two, and fell out, saying, "Lord, help me!"

In the hospital, I woke up, and they said, "Stop fighting; you're alright." They had opened my chest with one cut from the solar plex down through my belly button, and one cut from one arm pit to the next armpit, with over 150 staples in my chest.

I walked out after two weeks with my right kidney gone. I then got a job working at Greyhound Trailways. Sometimes I worked the drive, and sometimes I worked sending the luggage up to those on the drive.

I met this girl. She was nineteen, and I was twenty-seven, and we got married. I had two boys and a girl. She didn't want to break her family ties. Seeing it would be hard to raise them, I left the children with her and got the divorce.

Then I went to Phoenix, Arizona, where I was writing a book a publisher wanted in San Diego, but when I got there, the Lord said he wanted me to preach it, so I scrapped the whole idea.

That's where I found crack cocaine in Phoenix. This stuff was so addicting, and I always wanted more, so I sold my car and spent some money on crack but also bought a bus ticket back from there to Houston and back to Omaha. In Omaha, I started using crack cocaine.

I remember trying to rob a bookstore, and when I asked for the money, he said, "No." I thought, "He's not supposed to say 'no.' Let me get the hell out of here," so I walked down the sidewalk, but he came from behind me and held me till the police came. I did a flat year for that!

After I got out, not long after, I went back out again. I had a car, so I went from Quik Trip to Quik Trip, taking cases of pop down to the jitney stand, selling twenty dollars' worth of pop, and using the money to buy crack till they caught up with me and my ex on 84th and L Street.

After that, I went out one last time before I had a stretch of clean time. I was on a binge, and my ex and I came to the glass blowing place. She said they had a tip jar, so I told her to distract them while I grabbed the tip jar. So she did, and I grabbed the tip jar and ran with it. While I was running, they were catching up with me; I stumbled and fell on the jar. It broke, the money went everywhere, and I said, "Let me get the hell out of this place."

As I ran toward 16th and Cummings, three squad cars converged on me, telling me to lay on my face. "We've got guns on you."

So, they arrested me, but there was a silver lining in all of this. While I was in booking, a social worker came up to me and said, "We have a program for people who have mental illness and substance abuse problems. If you stay clean a year, the charges will be dropped."

I thought to myself, "It sure beats being in jail."

A year later, I was still clean, and the charges were dropped. Channel 7 interviewed me for this. I was at Earl Brown's 3/4-way house on Florence and Lothrop. From March 2006 till 2018, I stayed clean. In 2019, I relapsed;, but now I am a year clean from crack cocaine in August. I'm almost three months sober from alcohol. Alcohol is a drug! I switched addictions to alcohol from crack cocaine.

We all have to overcome our food addiction through fasting to bring the Spirit of Christ into our body.

I'm going to get the laugh last because I surrendered to Alcoholics Anonymous, growing along spiritual lines. I am gaining the capacity to be honest. God showed me that if I handle my body by yielding it as a living sacrifice. Sacrifices were what the law was teaching us, that we have a spiritual life-style, where Christ is the perfect sacrifice, the spiritual, divine training to offer your contact with God through the stomach, forgoing eating to gain spiritual contact. Now I have one day at a time to drink only! "For by one Spirit are we all baptized into one body whether we be Jews or Gentiles whether we be bond or free and have all made to drink into one Spirit" (1 Cor. 12:13).

Laugh Best

THE LAST SHALL be first; and the first shall be last. For many are called, but few are chosen. My race has suffered more than any other race. God made us last in the beginning that we might be first in the end. Laugh best. "Standfast in the liberty where with Christ has made us free and be not entangled again with the yolk of bondage" (Gal. 5:1).

I am free to live life on life's terms and drink only; no food into your stomach because that is where the contact is. Yea freedom from your stomach were which eating and eating. "Man shall not live by bread alone; but by every word that proceedeth out of the mouth of God!" (Luke 4:4).

I am not eating every time my stomach says feed me. No. "Be not conformed to this world but be yea transformed by the renewing of your mind; that ye may prove what is that good, acceptable, and perfect will of God" (Rom. 12:2).

"I am going to reach full capacity about spirituality as I hunger and thirst after righteousness shall be filled" (Matt. 5:6).

"Neither be ye sorry for the joy of the Lord is your strength" (Neh. 8:10).

Display Treatment

DISPLAY TREATMENT IS why I am writing this book. I have realized that true sobriety isn't without a real transformation in the said person's spirit to God's Spirit. All must admit to find in their innermost self that they have a problem. If said individual wants sober living, which can lead to godly living through his personal Spirit, which is Christ, through fasting, you not only cover all the steps but can gain eternal life by crossing over to the Spirit of God dwell in you now if any man have not the Spirit of Christ; he is none of His" (Rom. 8:9).

> Behold, the days came, saith the Lord, that I will make a new covenant with the house of Israel, and with the house of Judah: Not according to the covenant that I made with their fathers in the day when I took them by the hand to bring them out of the land of Egypt; which my covenant they brake, although I was an husband unto them, saith the Lord. But this shall the covenant that I will make with the house of Israel; after

those days, saith the Lord, I will put my law in their inward parts, and write them in their hearts; and will be their God and they shall be my people. And they shall not teach no more every man his neighbor saying, know the Lord for they shall all know me, from the least of them unto the greatest of them, saith the Lord: for I will forgive their iniquity, and I will remember their sin no more (Jer. 31:31–34).

For where is man's spirit that would connect with God? "The spirit of man is the candle of the Lord, searching all the inward parts of the belly" (Prov. 20:27). That's the place food addiction has taken us to. You can cross over to eternal life when you're ready to fast (starve yourself) to get to Him; only clear liquids in your body non-stop for forty days and nights in a row!

Only his people know about crossing over to eternal life through the belly! Our food addiction has to stop. Even going without meat in your diet is good because anytime you eat meat, you'll break or stop God from drawing up your stomach! To heavenly places in Christ Jesus!

All your character defects won't be mentioned. Your sins and iniquity will be forgotten through this type of spiritual worship. Eating is natural; drinking only is spiritual. You're dying to your flesh, but through liquids, your stomach (spirit) is getting stronger day by day till you reach forty days and nights consecutively. The liquids change into His Spirit at that time. Only people who have been converted through His will are going to make it or cross over.

Display treatment is all about action if I want to maintain sobriety. I don't want to be sober and miss out on eternal life. We displayed treatment in the biblical sense, but it all starts with being sober! For those who want to really lay down their lives for the ultimate prize, we must overcome our food addiction to identify with his holy type of lifestyle. Every time your stomach is empty and growls, you head for whatever wets your whistle; not so in Christ. Grab water or a clear liquid like apple juice or the like, and now you're following Christ.

You must first admit that you have a problem. I admitted to others about crack cocaine but not about alcohol until something came into my mind, saying, "You can handle beer" through to myself I know I have trouble with the hard stuff yea, I can handle beer.

I tried one can of Colt 45–24 oz., and it didn't bother me. Then I had one in the morning and one at night, and that didn't bother me either. Then I went to two cans of 24 oz. cans in the morning, and that got me really giddy; that was it for the morning till I had two in the morning and one at night, and then I was really loose. So I went to two cans in the morning and two cans at the night; now I was high!

I saw the pattern developing like it did with crack cocaine, so I thought I better quit before I do lose all control or get in a wreck. In fact, I did get into two wrecks, and both were my fault. My insurance premium doubled, then sometime after that, I told my sponsor that I relapsed on beer. Now I know that alcohol is a drug; I have to stay free from all mood and mind-altering substances; complete abstinence.

I checked into treatment and found out that I'm an alcoholic and an addict. Alcohol is what brought me into treatment this time, and I finally found out where I belong. That's why I am writing this book, so somebody might understand and a light might come on. "Let your light so shine before men, that they may see your good works and glorify your Father which is in Heaven" (Matt. 5:16).

Like it did for me, and I want not only sobriety but also eternal life. All I have to do is fast. That's all there is to it. I have to give my body back to God as a sacrifice; a living sacrifice holy acceptable unto God which is just my reasonable service (Rom. 12:1).

My starting place is my program that I work one day at time. I can eat, but I have to remember my spirit man inside. The first thing I stopped was eating meat; meat has got to stop being in my diet. Meat breaks your spirit from being drawn up, which we already proved is in your belly from Proverbs 20:27.

I have started a new life in these rooms and personal commitment to the Father. I'm going to do what people rarely do in sobriety, cross over to worship God in the Spirit and in truth. I'm taking my spirituality up a notch with fasting. I'm hoping that somebody in these rooms will follow my lead because "God is a Spirit, and they that worship the Father must worship Him in Spirit and in truth," which means I have to go days and weeks without food, not only for myself but for others in this category who are outside these rooms and want a powerful, moving message, one where you can say that God visited us this day or this night. We're going to the top of Mt. Sion (Rev. 14:1); there are going to be 144,000 men with me, and I don't know how God is going to do it. It might be through this book. It might be through somebody hearing me. One thing I do know is, "it's not by might nor by power; but by my Spirit saith the Lord unto Zerubbabel" (Zech. 4:6).

I learned what some of my triggers are: self-pity, anger, anxiety, and H.A.L.T.: Hunger, Anger, Lonely, and Tired; old playgrounds, playmates, playthings, money, bars, clubs, women, sex, and depression are also on the list. Parties is one too—birthdays, and holidays. There are more, I'm sure, but this is a rough sketch. Getting a job, not a getting a job, and broken promises; all these are triggers for me. When they pop up, I have to be on guard, but when I fast, my mind is on getting through that without eating or putting anything in my body whatsoever. It's easier because the more I focus on the pure spirit I'm trying to get, it gives me the lift I need to make it just one more day. You have to be chosen by God to do these things. "Many are called out few are chosen" (Matt. 22:14).

Is God speaking to you about spiritual matters?

Alcohol was just my springboard into a life that really worships God our Father by gaining his physician presence through fasting. I started slow now, and I have been twice out forty days and nights without food, just clear liquids.

I am just like Jericho; the walls had to come down in defeat: alcohol and cocaine addiction. But he has created all things beautiful in his time. Jericho became admired and a city where Christ didn't have any trouble in modern-day Jericho. All he did was to pass right through, and those who were ordained to follow. He did miracles nigh unto Jericho and leaving Jericho, but in the city proper, everything and everybody was in order. Imagine how Christ was impressed with Jericho that had the right spirit.

We can also receive His Spirit if we want to live a cross-over lifestyle. All it take is for the individual to want all that God has to offer. God is pulling a church amidst those who are spiritually chosen of the Father and to give their bodies to Him by having His name written in their foreheads. I feel there are 144,000 men coming out of the rooms. It's not for them who need it; it's for them who want it. Everybody needs Christ, but not everybody wants Christ. You have to be predestinated!

DISPLAY TREATMENT
A Perfect Stranger

WHAT WOULD I tell a perfect stranger? You can diagnose yourself if you are one of us. Try doing some controlled drinking; it won't take much to decide whether you can drink like a gentleman or not. A perfect stranger who picks up this book can see something in the book that relates to whatever level of the Spirit you're on at this time. I'm trying to reach full capacity to be honest. Some have grave emotional and mental disorders, but many of them do recover if they have the capacity to be honest. My job is to be honest. My job is to get to the full capacity. "They that wait upon the Lord shall renew their strength they shall mount up with wings as eagles; then shall and run and not be weary; they shall walk and not faint" (Isa. 40:31).

A perfect stranger sees an overcomer centering his life to be of maximum service to anyone who reads this book. A perfect stranger will find that God has taken me from the pit of hell to enlightening me to write this book. I'm at full capacity, now if you're newer than or older than me. I'm an orphan who was given to the state of Michigan when I was two years old. When my father and mother forsake me, the Lord will take me up (Ps. 27:10).

A perfect stranger will think this is different. If you're not letting God in because you have your walls up, I pray that God brings down your walls by any means necessary. Jericho received him and was the only city he didn't spend his virtue to heal; they were straight. He passed right through the city.

Once we find time to give back, this book will let you see Mt. Sion, the holy mountain of God, and fasting for forty days and nights in a row are doable. The 144,000 men horsing around are going to get serious and take the mountain by storm. They're going to get the laugh last. Laugh's best. So, the last shall be first and the first last, for many are called but few chosen (Matt. 20:16).

God made us last from the beginning so we could be first in the end. It all starts with a desire to stop drinking. I'm glad a perfect stranger just might cross over get the real prize eternal life; you must be hard on yourself but considerate of others. God bless.

CPSIA information can be obtained
at www.ICGtesting.com
Printed in the USA
BVHW042045200223
658864BV00002B/39